Discovering Psalms as Prayer

How we can use the Psalms morning, noon and night

Rev Andy Roland

Foreword by Rev David Runcorn

Author of Choice, Desire and the Will of God,
Spirituality Workbook, Space for God etc.

Published by Filament Publishing Ltd
16, Croydon Road, Waddon, Croydon Surrey CR0 4PA

Printed by IngramSpark

ISBN 978-1-911425-90-8

Drawing of the Syrian Orthodox Cross, or Thomas Cross, used throughout the book
This is taken from the most ancient Christian sculptures in India, c. 8th century C.E. The dove represents the Holy Spirit. The cross has leaves showing it is the Tree of Life. At the foot of the cross come out four rivers, referring to the four rivers that came out of the Garden of Eden, as in Genesis 2.10-14. It is also possible that they represent the lotus flower, but I personally doubt it. The whole symbol speaks to me of Jesus' proclamation at the Feast of Tabernacles:

> *On the last day of the festival, the great day, while Jesus was standing there, he cried out, "Let anyone who is thirsty come to me, and let the one who believes in me drink. As the scripture has said, 'Out of the believer's heart shall flow rivers of living water.'" Now he said this about the Spirit, which believers in him were to receive; for as yet there was no Spirit, because Jesus was not yet glorified." (John 7.37-39)*

Contents

Contents

Foreword

At the heart of the bible is a collection of prayers, songs, poems and reflections called the Book of Psalms. They express every mood, dilemma and longing of life. From deepest love to angry protest they address God, themselves and the world and always with fresh and startling honesty. 'All of life is there'. There was a deep and practical wisdom that led Hebrew and early Christians to shape their daily praying around the regular reciting of the psalms.

This is a discipline that has been lost in our times and our prayers are the poorer for that. In Discovering Psalms as Prayer Andy Roland weaves together the wisdom of a faithful, personal pilgrimage with practical guidance for reading the psalms. It will be a gift to those wanting to make that discovery for themselves.

We are in his debt.

Rev David Runcorn

"I always pray at sea, never on land."

Sir Francis Chichester, round-the-world yachtsman.

Chapter 1

The Problem of Prayer

In one of their classic sketches, Dudley Moore asked Peter Cook about prayer:

Dud   *'Ere, Pete, d'you pray"*

Pete   *Yeah, Dud, I pray, if I want something, like. Like, if I'm ill and I want to get better so I can see the footie on Tuesday I say, "God, if you're there, please listen to me. If you're not, don't bother. But if you are, please let me get better by Tuesday, and I'll believe in you and go to church and all that." 'Course, if you do get better by Tuesday, you don't know if it's God's what's done it or if you'd have got better in any case.*

Dud   *Yeah, I know, it's difficult.*

Dud has a point. Prayer is difficult. And mysterious.

How do I know if I am praying? Do I kneel or stand or sit or lie prostrate? Do I say words out loud or say them in my head or not use words at all? Am I alone or with my wife or with loads of other people? Am I in a special place like a church or am I at home or walking the dog? Am I asking Someone to heal my wife's cancer or just enjoying a sunset? The answer to all these is, yes, possibly.

There are two main components to prayer, talking and listening. Both have problems attached. (I am not going to consider other modes of prayer, e.g. gazing, holding, dancing etc.)

Talking

When we talk in prayer, we are often asking for things, for ourselves or for other people. But what are we actually doing? We are saying or thinking words, and there is no one else actually there. Yet it doesn't feel as if we are talking to ourselves. It's a bit like posting a letter or sending an email. You have communicated to someone, but there is no evidence yet of anyone receiving it. A common complaint about prayer is that one's words keep "bouncing off the ceiling".

Is it in fact a form of madness, just as talking to oneself is seen as a sign of madness? Even if God is real, if there is no perceptible interchange, does the charge of madness still stick? I don't think so, simply because when you see someone muttering to thmselves on the street, they seem completely cut off from the people around them, while my experience is that any form of prayer acts to connect me better with those around me.

But what about asking for things, like the healing of someone dear to us from a terminal disease? Is it not at the very least presumptuous of us to pray a few prayers and expect the laws of the universe to crumple at our verbal onslaught? Perhaps the instrument of effective prayer is not our words, but the degree to which our lives are surrendered to God and so be able to be a clearer channel for his will. And perhaps what we think of as a supreme tragedy may look different from the other side of eternity.

Archbishop William Temple (1881-1944) was asked if prayer worked. He replied, *"When I pray coincidences happen, and when I don't they don't."*

I think that the purpose of words in prayer is primarily the need to be honest – with the One beyond us and also with ourselves. If what is killing us is the terminal diagnosis one's wife has just received, then not to voice it is a supreme act of dishonesty. If on the other hand what is uppermost is the need for a parking space, then if that is where we are, that is the prayer we should pray. Over time we will hopefully be taught to live life at a deeper level.

One of my favourite prayers comes in the American comedy "Tin Men" (marvellous, about a feud between two aluminum siding salesmen, do watch it). Danny de Vito is at a salad bar in the Smorgasbord Restaurant and prays.

Tilley lifted his eyes to the ceiling.

"God," he murmured, "if you're responsible for all this stuff down here, maybe you've got a moment's attention for me... Between the IRS, this Home Improvement Commision and Mr Maringay, I got it up to here with this bullshit. To be frank with you, I'm in the toilet here. If you can see your way -"

He was interrupted by a woman with a tray who was attempting to reach over him.

"Listen, I'm praying here ... go around."

"I wanted to get some salad," she said indignantly.

"It's out of order... go around.... Do what you can, all right? I appreciate it. Amen."

(Tin Men by Martin Noble p.118)

It's a great prayer because it starts with worship (contemplating the salad bar and lifting his eyes upwards), telling the truth, (I'm in the toilet here), and ends with thanks, (I appreciate it). Maybe a little less self-centredness would not go amiss, (I'm praying here... go around), but we all struggle with that.

And if you watch the movie you will see that the prayer is answered, but in a very upside-down way.

It seems to me that whatever else prayer does, it changes our internal landscape. When I was 18 I made a major commitment of my life to God. (I did this by going to Woolworths on Monday morning and buying a rug and an alarm clock so as to get up in the morning to pray). When I reflected that all this faith stuff was probably imaginary, I had three lines of defence:

1. As a historian I considered Mark's gospel as a reliable, effectively first-hand account of the ministry of Jesus; therefore presumably he did rise from the dead, therefore presumably God exists.

2. I found that when I prayed in the morning, I went through the day in a much more centred and effective way; I could not believe that the universe was so chaotic that one part of it worked better (i.e. me) on the basis of what was not in fact the case.

3. I deeply believed, and still believe, that I am *not* the summit of human spiritual achievement (as if!) – there are countless others who know more and better and deeper than me.

We talk as if we are talking to God (or Higher Power or Allah or the Eternal One), because talking is how we express ourselves, and we do that in the faith that *"closer is He than breathing, and nearer than hands and feet"*. (Tennyson)

As Mahatma Gandhi said, *"Prayer is not asking. It is a longing of the soul. It is daily admission of one's weakness. It is better in prayer to have a heart without words than words without a heart."*

But what can we do when our words are too thin?

Listening

Rabbi Lionel Blue wrote, *"Prayer is when God speaks to us."*
(To Heaven with Scribes and Pharisees)

This statement thrusts us into a radically new way of thinking
about prayer. Our words become less significant, but
the problem of prayer is intensified. If I cannot judge the
significance of the words I actually say in prayer, how on earth
can I say anything about the silence which is all I hear?

Feelings

It is possible that in prayer we experience strong feelings
which we might interpret as the presence of God. But how
can we distinguish between a communication from God to
our inner self, and a self-manufactured emotion? Are we just
indulging in self-hypnosis? As Dud said, *"It's difficult"*.

I remember hearing a story of St Teresa of Avila (1515-1582).
One of her nuns rushed up to her in great excitement, saying
*"Mother, I have just had a most wonderful experience of
God's love while praying in the chapel!"* *"Never mind, my
daughter,"* the saint replied. *"Go back to your prayers and it
will soon go away."*

Thoughts

Perhaps God speaks within us, through our thoughts.

John Wimber, a remarkable American pastor who founded
the Vineyard Churches and expected every Christian to pray
for healing, encouraged everyone to listen to the Holy Spirit
speaking to them. At one of his conferences I attended, he
was asked what hearing the Holy Spirit was like. He replied,
"It's a hunch."

This is similar to the concept of prayer set out in Alcoholics Anonymous. On p. 86 Bill Wilson wrote, *"On awakening let us think about the twenty-four hours ahead... In thinking about our day we may face indecision... Here we ask God for inspiration, an intuitive thought or a decision. We relax and take it easy... We are often surprised how the right answers come after we have tried this for a while. What used to be the hunch or the occasional inspiration gradually becomes a working part of the mind."*

My own experience is that several times I have received an answer to a problem through my thoughts while praying. The thought always seems to have a particular quality about it. A fresh idea comes to me, one that I had not thought of before, but once there it seems blindingly obvious. Either it is the Holy Spirit communicating in me, or else my subconscious is a much more interesting place than I had suspected.

Non-Thoughts

Finally there is the form of prayer which uses neither words nor feelings nor thoughts, a form of prayer which in the east is called meditation and in the western church contemplation. (At which point Dud and Pete walk off in disgust).

A classic decsription comes in "The Cloud of Unknowing", an anonymous book written in the 14th century in Northanptonshire, England.

"When you first begin, you find only darkness, and as it were a cloud of unknowing. You don't know what this means except that in your will you feel a simple steadfast intention reaching out towards God. Do what you will, this darkness and this cloud remains between you and God... Reconcile yourself

to wait in this darkness as long as necessary, but still go on longing after him whom you love.

"By love may he be gotten and holden; by thought never."

This is comparable to some extent to Buddhist and Hindu meditation, and to the modern practice of mindfulness. They can be both a preparation for and a goal of prayer. My friend David Goymour reports:

"I have practised meditaiton for about 45 years. Practice is patchy; there have been patches when I have neglected it, but I have always come back to it... In the last 10+ years I have become increasingly aware that meditation is important to me, a spiritual anchor. The curious thing about it is that as I sit down and prepare myself to meditate, each time is unique. It always has a fresh, unexpected quality. It can be hard work, battling with the mind, keeping it fixed on the mantra. Sometimes it is just very natural. What you can't see is what it is doing in the central nervous system. At the end of the half hour, when I open my eyes, I almost invariably have a deeper sense of being myself. Philosophical writings from Plato onwards tell us that this immortal invisible consciousness is the Self. Meditation puts us in touch with the universal Self... As I continue to meditate, I get more and more convinced of the reality of Some Power greater than and beyond myself."

Houston, we have a problem

The key problem with prayer is that we have a problem with it. As soon as we say to ourselves, *"I think I'll pray now"*, we (or at any rate, I) are/am faced with an immediate sense of reluctance. It's like starting the car and trying to drive it with the handbrake on (as I have frequently tried to do – it doesn't work very well). It is, I believe, a common experience that as soon as I think about praying, a host of other thoughts crowd in – I need a cup of tea/coffee first; I need a bit more sleep; baby, it's cold outside; No! I've got too many things to do! and, What on earth am I doing?

The Hindu scripture, the Bhagavad Gita (Song of God) has this wonderful verse:

> *The mind is resless, Krishna, impetuous, self-willed, hard to train;*
> *to master the mind seems as difficult as to master the mighty winds.*

(Bhagavad Gita ch.6 v. 34)

So we need a strategy.

Some strategies

When I was a teenager, and part of St Matthew's Youth Club in Rugby, the standard formula for prayer was ACTS – Adoration, Confession, Thanksgiving, Supplication. I tried it but did not find it too helpful – it all felt a bit forced for me.

One excellent strategy was told me by Robin Smith, a chaplain at Lee Abbey, a wonderful Christian holiday centre in North Devon – do Google it. I went to talk to him about how hard I found it to pray in any consistent way. His advice was *"Try to pray two minutes a day."* I remember leaving, thinking, *"Huh, that's not much,"* but of course he was quite right. The way to avoid the poison of legalism is to have a rule that is an invitation to go further, not a rule that one is constantly trying to achieve and either failing in, or succeeding in, with the risk of developing a pink glow of self-righteousnoess.

Around 1966 I visited the Mayflower Centre in East London, a flagship Christian community centre in a very deprivd area of Canning Town. George Burton was the leader of the Centre from 1959 and a completely down-to-earth bloke, whose philosophy was summed up in the book he wrote, "People Matter More Than Things". I heard him talk about prayer. *"If you don't know what to pray, say the Lord's Prayer. If you still don't know what to pray, say it again – it's the prayer Jesus gave us."* Simple and easy advice which I appreciated, but one which I did not particularly practise.

A useful strategy, for those who are familiar with church, is that of St Anthony of the Desert. Anthony was born in Roman Egypt about 251 AD. When he was 18 both his parents died, leaving him a sister to look after. One Sunday he arrived late, in the middle of the gospel reading, (I relate to that), and heard the words of Jesus *"Go, sell everything you have, and give it to the poor."* He felt that this was a word addressed directly to him. (It seems that God often uses the Bible to speak like this). He did just that. He sold everything, apart from what was needed to support his sister, and became a hermit, dedicating his life to prayer and moving eventually to the Egyptian desert. He lived to over a hundred, dying in 356. Shortly afterwards, St Athanasius, Bishop of Alexandria, wrote his life story. In it Anthony gives this advice to those wanting to live a spiritual life:

"Pray continually; avoid vain-glory, sing psalms before sleeping and on awaking."

(Life of St Anthony by St Athanasius, section 55).

I have found this good advice. Though I do not sing psalms, there are a number of hymns that I can sing (quietly!) to commit the night to God and to welcome the morning, helping me to attune myself to the idea of praying.

The Bible is a great resource. Every time we open it we participate in a conversation between man and God, or between man and man about God. This can help take us out of our everyday concerns. This is especially true if we allow enough time to let the words resonate inside us. I assume other scriptures can do that as well, such as the Upanishads and the Bhagavad Gita of Hinduism, the Qu'ran of Islam; and the Dhammapada of Buddhism. All of these assert that there is One who is beyond this world and to whom we can open ourselves.

But none of these strategies I find work as well for me as that particular bit of the Bible called the Psalms.

Really?

"For years I avoided the book of Psalms...
with uncanny consistency I would land on a psalm
that aggravated, rather then cured my problem..."

Philip Yancey "The Bible Jesus Read".

Chapter 2

The Problem with Psalms

I t is clear that, as this is a book about the Psalms, I consider them a Good Thing. But before we get on to how I discovered that the Psalms were a Good Thing, let me start with how they can at first be rather a Problem.

When I spoke to my publisher, Chris Day, about my idea of writing about the psalms, he was enthusiastic. He told me of the problems he had encountered in trying to get to grips with them.

"A few years ago I tried to get to know the psalms by reading a couple of pages on a daily basis, a bite-size chunk every

day. I thought, there's got to be a little treasure here for me to discover. I did not know them, other than chanting them from time to time in church using the Daily Missal. And then they were in a kind of musical straitjacket. But I found it heavy going. The translation may not have helped, because I only had quite an archaic version with me. I realise now that I read them without context, without any explanation. It would have been nice to understand a little bit about them, the references to people, places and events. I look forward to what you are going to write."

What was Chris's problem?

The first problem is that there is no narrative. Most of the other books of the Bible have a clear narrative. X happened followed by Y. It's not hard to get one's compass bearings. But with the psalms, it is just one blessed thing after another, with no ongoing story. And with wildly different lengths. One psalm is just two verse long, Psalm 117; Psalm 118 has 29 verses and Psalm 119 has 176!

The second problem is the emotional content. Praise, lament and revenge are all mixed up, often in the same psalm. Take psalm 3 for example:

verse 3:   *But you, O Lord, are a shield around me,*
               my glory, and the one who lifts up my head.
And verse 7: *You strike all my enemies on the cheek;*
               you break the teeth of the wicked.

It can be confusing. And downright disturbing. Psalm 137 stars off beautifully, and became a famous pop song in the 1970s:

     By the rivers of Babylon -
     there we sat down and wept
     when we remembered Zion.

But it ends horribly:
>O daughter of Babylon, you devastator!...
>Happy shall they be who take your little ones
>and dash them against the rock!

The third problem is the references to long-forgotten history, e.g. Psalm 83. Who were Edom, the Ishmaelites, Moab, the Hagrites, Gebal, Ammon, Amalek, Philistia, Tyre, Assyria and Lot?

And yet there are spiritual riches tucked away in the most unlikely psalms, such as Psalm 36:9:
>With you is the fountain of life;
>in your light do we see light.

For first 38 years of my life, psalms did not form part of my personal spiritual diet, even though I was quite familiar with them because they were an integral part of Anglican worship. I had attended church since the age of 8, when I was sent to boarding school. In the summer term the whole school went to Dunchurch parish church on Sunday mornings. At that time the standard Sunday service was Morning Prayer or Matins at 11.00, with Evensong at 6.30, and this pattern continued in the churches I attended up to my mid 30's. (The movement to make Parish Communion or the Eucharist the main Sunday service had started in the 1950's, but did not take over virtually all parish churches until about 1980).

There were a lot of psalms in Anglican worship then. Morning Prayer would start with Psalm 95, followed by two or three psalms. Then followed a reading from the Old Testament followed by an ancient canticle, "Te Deum Laudamus" (the Latin of the opening words, appropriately similar to "Tedium"), a New Testament reading and another canticle, the Benedictus, from Luke 1.68-79. All of these would be chanted, accompanied by the organ and choir. Each verse was split into two halves, with a long note covering most of the half verse, ending the line with a short tune of 3, 4 or 5 notes. Nowadays you mostly have to go to a cathedral to hear it. Or listen to Anglican chant on youtube.

I definitely know Psalm 95 by heart because I sang it most Sundays for about 30 years. It is a good test case for the psalms. It is called the Venitē, after the title in the Prayer Book "Venite Exultemus", Latin for "Come let us exult". It begins well:

> "O come, let us sing unto the Lord:
> Let us heartily rejoice in the strength of our salvation...
> For he is the Lord our God:
> and we are the people of his pasture, and the sheep
> of his hand."

But it goes on in verse 8 as follows:

> "Today if ye will hear his voice, harden not your hearts:
> as in the provocation and as in the day of temptation in
> the wilderness."

And it ends at verse 11:

> "Unto whom I sware in my wrath:
> that they shoiud not enter into my rest."

Ouch!

In modern versions of Morning Prayer, the last four verses are omitted. I am torn as to whether this is right, beause they are pretty downbeat, or whether they should be included so as to bring a dose of realism into our worship.

And then came the psalms of the day. These were literally
"of the day". Thomas Cranmer, Archbishop of Canterbury
under Henry VIII and Edward VI, was passionate about putting
Christian worship into the language of the people. In 1539
an English Bible was placed in every parish church, and in
1544 Cranmer wrote an English prayer of intercession, called
the Litany. After the death of Henry VIII, who had been a
religious conservative (provided it didn't cost him any money),
Cranmer organised the Book of Common Prayer, published
1549, with a more Protestant revision in 1552. He envisaged
that every parish church would have morning and evening
prayer every day. They were to replace the seven daily services
which had been said in the monasteries, abolished fifteen
years previously. The monks had followed a scheme of psalm
reading dating back more than a thousand years in which
all the psalms would have been sung or recited each and
every week. Cranmer lightened the load by going through
the psalms every month. This still happens in catherals up
and down the country. I am writing this on 19th January. Thus
today you would have heard/sung Psalms 95, 96 and 97 in
the morning, and Psalms 98, 99, 100 and 101 in the evening.
And you would have heard them in the translation of Miles
Coverdale who produced the Great Bible of 1539. (He did not
know Hebrew, so the Psalms were translated from Latin and
German translations – but he was a master of English prose).

It is by no means a bad way to use the psalms in daily
corporate worship. One priest described it as "roughage",
a bit like eating up your vegetables – good for you if not
immediately enjoyable.

However, it certainly did not speak to my condition. To learn
how the psalms could do that, I had to travel to India.

"What is the monastic charism? Simply put, it is to seek God with an undivided heart."

From the guest leaflet of Kurisumala Ashram.

Chapter 3

Kurisumala Ashram

The bus bounced along the narrow uphill roads, chugging up from the coastal plain of Kerala to the mountainous Western Ghats. At Pala it had to stop for emergency repairs, so I changed to another bus going to Eratupetta, and then on to the one for Vagamon which would drop me a kilometre from the ashram. On the way I read the Indian Express, (a newsaper in English). Here are some stories that struck me:

A resident in an up-market suburb of Calcutta was annoyed by street traders moving into his neighbourhood. Complaints to the police got him nowhere, so he offered a bribe to a local policeman, who replied, "Sir, you give me only for one day, but these people do so everyday. How can I do it?"

At a village festival in Calcutta a man came under the spell of the serpent deity Manasa and beheaded four people in the crowd. The police arrested eight people. (Why eight??)

There was a major article attacking a proposal to build a nuclear power station in Kerala. "The failure on the organisational front cannot be covered up with the use of more sophisticated technology. That will only result in more sophisticated failures."

There are 60,000 temple prostitues in Kerala, Maharashta and Karnataka, (southern Indian states), through poor families marrying their daughters to "trees or effigies".

Sri Ramakrishna, a major figure in the renaissance of Hinduism in the 19th century, said: "One yogi may believe any fantastic story of God's deeds, holding   that nothing is impossible to the omnipotent. Another may discount such tales. This is an attitude of the mind."

He also said: "The essence of all jnana sadhana (meditative wisdom) is love of God. Deep "bhakti" (devotion) will itself generate wisdom and dispassion."

These printed stories give a flavour of being in India. I was constantly in a position where I thought I knew what was happening, only to have the rug pulled from under my feet. And all this while on the way to one of the most significant spiritual encounters of my life.

This was in 1983, when I was halfway my theological training at Durham University. I was spending 9 weeks of the summer vacation in India, based at the Tamil Theological Seminary at Madurai, with the general question in my mind of what could/should Christianity look like when the surrounding culture is Indian rather than Western European.

Madurai was a very good place in which to reflect on this. Madurai is one of the seven key pilgirmage centres for Hinduism with a celebrated temple devoted to Shiva, the god of creation, destruction and regeneration. The city is in the centre of Tamil Nadu, a large southern Indian state, whose capital is Chennai, formerly Madras. It was never conquered by Moslems so its Hindu culture is untouched, with most people being vegetarian. It has its own distincitve langauge,Tamil, very different from Sanskrit. and a 288 letter aphabet. In the 17th Century the Jesuit missionary, Roberto de Nobili, adopted the dress and title of sannyassin, someone who has renounced worldly goods to focus on spiritual growth, and mastered Sanskrit, Tamil and Telugu. In the 18th century Lutheran missionaries made a strong impact. In 1946 the Anglican, Methodist, Congregationalist and Presbyterian churches united to become the Church of South India; Tamil Theological Seminary serves this as well as the Lutheran Church.

Tamilnadu Theological Seminary, or TTS, has a strong emphasis on social justice. In the words of Dr Robinson, Principal when I visited, *"We see the evil in society at two levels, in poverty, diseases, sub-human way of living (prostitution) , and at the root we see an unjust socio-economic order characterised by expoitation, corruption and oppression."* (What is TTS? p.12). I was privileged to see the Slum Development Programme at work, when some women arrived to say that had been told their homes on the pavement were about to be bulldozed that day; we were able to stop that happening. I also stayed a day in the Rural Devlopment Programme, seeing how they encouraged health care, work training and water provision. I also took part in a service on Sunday in the prison, had a set of stoles made for me at Arulagam, a house run by TTS which rescued young women from prostitution, and visited another house where they provided dormitories for 36 old people with no means of support.

From this base I explored further south, to Kanya Kumari, or Cape Cormorin, the southern tip of India. I then travelled north through Kerala, in the south west of India, visiting poor fishing communities, many of them Christian, and hearing of their struggle against debt and exploitation. My aim was to reach Kurisumala Ashram.

Kurisumala Ashram had been recommended to me by Esther Muirhead. She and my mother had been good friends and members of the Peace Pledge Union in the 1930s. Esther was a Quaker, who went to India and engaged in social work there, ultimately receiving an M.B.E. She gave me an introduction to Father Francis, who had founded the Ashram in 1958. He and a fellow-monk Bede Griffiths were committed to found a monastery which was a genuinely Indian expression of faith. He decribed how it started:

"On the morning of our departure (In Advent 1956) from Tiruvalla for the Mountain of the Cross, we had received from Mar Athanasios the saffron robe which is the mark of "Sannyasa", the life of renunciation in India. We observed the simple habits of life customary among sannyasis, going barefoot, renouncing furniture, even sitting on the floor for

meals, eating with our hands, vegetarian food and sleeping on a mat." (Kurisumala means Cross Mountain; an ashram is an Indian hermitage or monastery).

On the bus from Erattupetta I met a member of the Kurisumala community. He had originally wanted to join the army, but a broken arm had blocked that avenue. He trained as a photographer for 9 months, but was persuaded by his parents to return to their farm and work on the land. Two years later he visited Kurisumala. He was attracted by the deep prayer he encountered there, and wanted to join the ashram. He had a struggle with his parents, who said, "Why don't you become a priest? It's a much easier life." But he persevered and did join the ashram, first as a shishya or aspirant for 6 months, then as a novice or sadhaka, spiritual seeker, for 3 years, then as a "Brahmachari" or student under vows for 6 years. He had almost finished the period of brahmachari and would soon take sannyas – renunciation, taking life vows as a monk, or sannyasin. I guess he is still there, part of the community of 20 sannyassin. As soon as we got to the ashram he started talking less and in a low voice so as not to disturb the quiet atmosphere.

The guest master took me to see Father Francis Acharya (Acharya means Teacher), a grey-haired man with a full beard, wearinng the orange robe of a sannyasi. He was exactly the same age as my father, 61. He was Swiss but eventually took Indian nationality. He was very human and spoke excellent English. He was very pleased to hear of Esther Muirhead, and of the question in my mind about Christianity in an Indian setting. We met again next morning and walked to the mediation rock, where there is a fantastic view down 4,000 feet and 20 miles away to the sea. He told me that he had learnt meditation at school. He was bright and would finish the maths exercises before anyone else. He asked the master if he could read a book when he had finished. He was told no, but the master advised him that, when he had finished, he should look out of the window he was sitting by, pick a flower or some other object and just look at it. He did that, it was boring but he perservered. Then suddenly one day the flower ceased being an object and became a presence.

Meals were taken in silence, sitting on the floor and eating with one's fingers, Indian-style. A book was read, in English at lunchtime and in Malayalam at supper. The eucharist (or Holy Qurbana) was celebrated in Malayalam at 6.00, very beautifully with Indian lamps and flowers and incense, and with a sense of genuine solemnity.

In the evening there was a Bible "satsang", meditation. The first evening the satsang was about trees: how all creation meditates on God and how we, like the trees, need the same spirit of *silent* service. The next evening the Bible satsang was all about meditation – how we need to be like bees, meditating in our hives then going out and getting the honey; not like butterflies, flying very actively from flower to flower but collecting nothing.

On my last morning I got up at 3.45 to go to the night vigils and morning prayer, which were fortunately in English. I was impressed by the deep silence between the four vigil prayers, and at the end of the morning prayer. The slightest double tap from the Acharya's knuckle was enough to bring the prayer peacefully to its conclusion.

By 10.00 I was back in the bustling town of Kottayam where I was about to see the annual Snake Boat Race.

What bizarrely I failed to note in my diary at the time was the impact of that morning prayer on me. The ashram uses the oldest Christian prayers in India, from the Syrian Orthodox Church. I was deeply impressed by the poetic beauty of the prayers. But what I found particularly meaningful was the three psalms which the Syrian Orthodox Church says each and every morning, and I immediately adopted them for myself.

"My experience over the years has taught me that the Morning Watch with God day by day is an unfailing secret of power, progress, purpose and peace."

Jack C Winslow "When I Awake".

Chapter 4

Bus-friendly Morning Prayer

The three psalms which are central to Syrian Orthodox morning prayers are psalms 51, 63 and 113.

Psalm 51 starts:

> *Have mercy on me, O God,*
> *according to your steadfast love;*
> *according to your abundany mercy*
> *blot out my transgressions.*

The natural ending is at verse 17:

> *The sacrifice acceptable to God is a broken spirit;*
> *a broken and contrite heart, O God, you will not despise.*

Psalm 63 starts:
> *O God, you are my God, I seek you,*
> *my soul thirsts for you,*
> *my flesh faints for you,*
> *as in a dry and weary land where there is no water.*

The natural ending is at verse 8:
> *My soul clings to you;*
> *your right hand upholds me.*

Psalm 113 starts and continues with the theme of praise:
> *Praise the Lord!*
> *Praise, O servants of the Lord,*
> *Praise the name of the Lord.*

For the first time in my life I encountered psalms as prayers which made immediate sense to me. These three psalms are a wonderful ladder, leading from confession through trust to praise. I started using them daily, and found that wherever I was spiritually, something in these three psalms would speak directly to my situation. And by using them every day, I quickly got to know them by heart. Within a fortnight I could pray them anywhere without the need of a book. My homeward journey to England started a fortnight after my visit to Kurisumala. I got an overnight coach from Madurai to Madras, a 12 hour journey, stopping every two or three hours for comort breaks. I managed to sleep from half past midnight to 5.00. I remember looking out of the slightly leaking window at the grey rainswept countryside when I woke, praying the three psalms by memory and feeling a real connection with God.

I finish each psalm with the standard Christian ending:
> *Glory to the Father and to the Son*
> *and to the Holy Spirit;*
> *as it was in the beginning, is now,*
> *and shall be for ever. Amen.*

I continued using Psalms 51:1-17, 63:1-8 and 113 every morning for the next two years. I did not get bored, but I felt that perhaps I should spread my wings a bit and use a wider range of psalms. Over a series of long coach journeys I combed the book of psalms for ones that would express the same emotional journey. I started with the six traditional psalms of repentance used in Roman Catholic liturgy and added some of the most well known psalms of trust such as psalms 27 and 103 (Robert Louis Stevenson's favourite). On Fridays I use two psalms which reflect Christ's crucifixion. In the end I had a fortnight's selection, which I have stuck with ever since. I aimed to balance the length of psalms so that each day's palms are roughly the same length, but every day they go through the same ladder of confession, trust and praise.

For instance, on Tuesday week 1 we move from Psalm 6:
> *O Lord, do not rebuke me in your anger,*
> *or discipline me in your wrath...*
> *My soul also is struck with terror,*
> *while you, O Lord - how long?*

to Psalm 27:
> *The Lord is my light and my salvation;*
> *whom shall I fear?*
> *The Lord is the stronghold of my life;*
> *of whom shall I be afraid? ...*
> *Teach me your way, O Lord,*
> *and lead me on a level path*

and finally to Psalm 100:
> *Make a joyful noise to the Lord, all the earth.*
> *Worship the Lord with gladness;*
> *come into his presence with singing.*

On Wednesday of week 1 we move from Psalm 130:
> *Out of the depths I cry to you, O Lord.*
> *Lord, hear my voice!*

to Psalm 103:
> *Bless the Lord, O my soul,*
> *and do not forget all his benefits—*
> *who forgives all your iniquity,*
> *who heals all your diseases...*

> *Bless the Lord, all his works,*
> *in all places of his dominion.*
> *Bless the Lord, O my soul.*

The services at Kurisumala had also deeply impressed me with the poetry of their prayers, many of them written by St Ephrem (306 – 373). Francis Acharya said, *"While Western Christianity excels in clarity of expression, pregnant brevity and dogmatic definitions, the East, and very much so the Christian Orient, prefers the language of poetry in which parable, symbol and even myth make the Mystery present to the devotee and often bring him closer to the spiritual realities."*

These prayers achieve a remarkable balance of praise and humility. For example, the introduction to morning prayer starts:

In the name of the Father and of the Son and of the
Holy Spirit,
one true God to whom be glory
and on us mercy and compassion for ever and ever.
Amen.

It ends ends with this marvellous prayer:

Creator of the morning,
who drives out the darkness
and brings light and joy to all creation:
create in us habits of virtue,
and drive away from us all
the darkness of sin.
With the light give us joy
by the glorious rays of your grace,
Lord our God for ever.

After the psalms I typically read a passage from the New
Testament, followed by five minute's (or longer) silent
meditation. The Lord's Prayer then leads into prayer for the
day ahead and for other people. The closing prayers begin:

Open your doors of mercy. Lord;
hear our prayer and have mercy upon our souls.
Lord of the morning and ruler of the seasons,
hear our prayer and have mercy upon our souls.
Shine on us , Lord, and make us light like the day;
let your light shine in our minds
and drive away the shadows of error and night...

Because the introductory and concluding prayers are so beautiful, I have found that I never got tired of them. I still use them daily when I get up – and that is after almost 35 years of continuous use. Because I know them virtually by heart, I don't need to analyze them, I can simply express myself through them. And together with a pocket New Testament and Psalms, or a kindle, I can do my morning prayers anywhere, anytime.

When I was a curate at St Leonard's, Streatham from 1984-87, I used this pattern for my personal prayers, and was also able to share it with others. Eve, a strong-minded lady of 80, said,

"No! I have never felt at ease with praying, although over the last few months it has been easier. Maybe it is my attitude of not always being in real touch with God. With Jesus Christ I feel in closer touch. Strange though it may seem, in the silence following the psalms and Bible reading, thoughts that come into my mind are more like prayer thoughts – rather than actual prayers. But I do feel approaching the thought of prayer is much easier. Psalm 113 I find very difficult, although I have diligently read it. Sometimes it does not raise me to any heights at all. (Psalm 113 ends with "He gives the barren woman a home, making her a joyful mother of children", and Eve was never married). Psalm 103 and 139, I do find help and comfort from them. A strange feeling of belonging emanates form these two. Psalm 51 is of course mostly one of repentance. These I find easy to read and gain some peace of mind. Psalm 63 is one of encouragement, and perhaps in that one God's strength and power comes through."

When I became vicar at All Saints, Hackbridge and Beddington Corner in 1994 I would say it in the Lady Chapel in the church at 9.00, and continued till I retired in 2015. Not only did it feel personal to me, it was also hospitable to others joining in. For much of the time in Hackbridge I was joined by Clive Bell, a church member of. This is how he remembers it:

"I joined the church in 2000 with Jenny and Barry (his mother and stepfather). We did the Alpha course and we all got confirmed in November. We took the three psalms on board, saying them in our own homes, then reading a scripture. It became a bit of a lifestyle, quite pivotal, especially Psalm 51. Praying about repentance, looking at ourselves and helping with self-evaluation, was good. It was a bridge connecting us to the Old Testament and New Testament. These psalms lay a good foundation, humbling ourselves and praising God for who he is.

"In 2002 I moved to a flat near the church and was able to come to morning prayer in church with Andy. I was working in retail, in a supermarket, and had a lot of night shifts in the first few years, so I was able to attend the morning prayers quite regularly. It helped me in the midst of life's turmoils to look at myself through the Gospel readings and Psalms, relating them to daily life. Often with my family, friends and work I could see parallels with what we read in the morning. Certain phrases stuck in my mind all day, and this helped me step back and conduct myself appropriately. It was very beneficial in a very stressful area, giving me space to think clearly.

"I think it is quite sad if Christians neglect the Psalms."

Note 1
The Morning Prayer can be found on page 43. It can be downloaded for free from a blog at bibleinbrief.org, in a form which can be copied as a 4 page A5 leaflet ie, 2 side of A4.

Note 2

In the Syrian Orthodox liturgy, unlike in the western church, the last two verses of Psalm 51 and the last three verses of psalm 63 are omitted. Psalm 51:18-19 refer to the Temple sacrifices; Psalm 63:9-11 are devoted to cursing one's enemies. Both of these passages take the focus off our own relationship with God and I do not find them helpful.

Note 3

The numbering of the psalms are taken from western Bibles which use the ancient Hebrew text. Roman Catholic and Eastern Orthodox Bibles use a slightly different numbering system based on the ancient Greek translation, the Septuagint.

Note 4

The prayers are taken from "Prayer with the Harp of the Spirit volume 1", first translated by Dom Bede Griffiths and published at Kurisumala in 1983. I have made a few changes. I do not include the "Hail Mary" because that is not my tradition. I have used versions of "Holy, holy, holy" etc. which are familiar to Anglicans. I included "Open your doors of mercy, Lord', ("the B'outho of Mar Jacob") from the service book of the Church of North India as I found it particularly poetic.

Morning Prayers
(Syrian Orthodox tradition in South India - abridged)

Introduction
In the name of the Father and of the Son and of the
Holy Spirit,
one true God to whom be glory
and on us mercy and compassion for ever and ever.
Amen.

Holy, holy, holy Lord
God of power and might,
Heaven and earth are full of your glory.
Hosanna in the highest.

Blessed is he who comes in the name of the Lord.
Hosanna in the highest.

Holy God,   )

Holy and strong,   ) three times
Holy and immortal,   )
have mercy on us.   )

Lord, have mercy upon us.
Lord, have pity and mercy upon us.
Lord, receive our service and our prayers
and have mercy upon us.

Glory to you, O God.
Glory to you, Creator,
Glory to you, Christ the King,
who have compassion on your sinful servants.
Bless, Lord.

The Lord's Prayer: Our Father, who art in heaven …

> Creator of the morning,
> who drives out the darkness
> and brings light and joy to all creation:
> create in us habits of virtue,
> and drive away from us all
> the darkness of sin.
> With the light give us joy
> by the glorious rays of your grace,
> Lord our God for ever. Amen

Psalms

	Week 1	Week 2
Monday	51.1-17; 63.1-8; 113	86, 96
Tuesday	6; 27; 100	25, 97
Wednesday	130; 103	102, 98
Thursday	32, 33	38, 36.5-9, 99
Friday	22, 138	69 (om. 22=28), 93
Saturday	40, 23, 146	143, 145
Sunday	95, 118	95, 66, 67

Bible meditation

A short Bible passage is read, e.g. from a Gospel, followed by some minutes' silent meditation.

Intercessions (Prayer for others)

Closing Prayers

> Open your doors of mercy. Lord;
> hear our prayer and have mercy upon our souls.
> Lord of the morning and ruler of the seasons,
> hear our prayer and have mercy upon our souls.

Shine on us, Lord, and make us light like the day;
let your light shine in our minds
and drive away the shadows of error and night.
The creation is full of light,
give your light also to our hearts
that we may praise you all the day long.
The morning and evening praise you, Lord,
they bring you the prayers of your Church.
Light which gives light to all creatures,
give light to our minds that we may thank you, Lord.

It is good to give thanks to the Lord,
to sing praise to your name, Most High,
to proclaim your goodness in the morning
and your faithfulness in the night.
Lord, in the morning, we pray, hear our voice.
In the morning we prepare ourselves to be with you.
Lord, have compassion on your people.
Lord, pardon and forgive the sins of us all.
Holy One, let your right hand rest upon us,
and pardon our weaknesses,
because your name is for ever. Amen.

"Evening, and morning, and at noon, will I pray, and cry aloud: and he shall hear my voice."

Psalm 55.17 - Authorised Version

Chapter 5

Midday Prayer - Into the Woods

F ive miles from Gatwick airport lies the small suburban
village of Crawley Down.

At the end of a smart cul de sac is a bumpy track which turns
into a narrow tarmac road, twisting its way through half a
mile of woodland to a series of low one storey buildings,
the Monastery of the Holy Trinity. This has been the home of
the Community of the Servants of the Will of God, a small
community of monks with the odd nun, since 1938.

It is a place of great tranquility and simplicity. Accomodation
is in a series of cells – single rooms with a bed, a table and

a chair, and an outside corridor leading to toilets. Meals are eaten in silence, apart from one talking meal per week. Greater silence lasts from the end of Vespers at 8.00pm to 9.30am the following morning. Lesser silence, during the day, means only talking if it is essential.

I have been going there on retreat for over 20 years. I try to go every two or three months for a couple of days. I love the peace of the place; it is often there I get my most creative ideas. But the absence of time presures brings its own pressure. So I am glad of the regular monastic services, called offices, that punctuate the day, providing a sense of structure. In times past, monasteries would have seven shortish services every day, following the verse in Psalm 119.164: "Seven times a day I praise you." These "offices" are:

> Matins – on waking up
> Lauds (meaning "praise") – at the start of the day
> Terce – mid-morning
> (Note: Terce, Sext and None come from the old Roman way of telling the time, before clocks were invented)
> Sext – noon
> None – mid-afternoon
> Vespers – at sundown
> Compline – on going to bed

This pattern was established over 1500 years ago by St Benedict of Nursia (480 – 543). He was a hermit who gradually gathered round him a community of fellow-monks, (After his first couple of communities tried to poison him) He wrote a rule of life which has been the framework for monasteries in western Europe ever since. Chapter 18 reads:

Psalm 118 having been completed, therefore, on two days, Sunday and Monday, let the nine Psalms from Psalm 119 to Psalm 127 be said at Terce, Sext and None, three at each Hour, beginning with Tuesday. And let these same Psalms be repeated every day until Sunday at the same Hours.

(Note: because of the difference between Protestant and Roman Catholic bibles, using Hebrew and Greek numbeirng respectively, Psalm 118 is actually Psalm 119, and Psalms 119 to 127 are Psalms 120 to 128. You can easily work out which is which. In most Bibles today Psalm 120 has 7 verses and Psalm 119 has 176!)

At Crawley Down this pattern is slightly shortened. Matins is at 4.00, but guests are not expected to get up for this one. Lauds is at 7.00. There is no Terce. Sext and None are said before and after lunch, at 12.00 and 1.45 respectively. (None has been dropped for the moment). Vespers, together with the Mass, is said after supper at 6.30. Compline is said privately.

I specially valued Sext and None. These were very short and simple, less than 15 minutes. A hymn is sung and three short psalms said. These come from the mini-collection of Psalms 120 to 128 called Songs of Ascents, probably pilgrimage songs sung as the pilgrims went up to Jerusalem. Then there is a short reading from the Community Rule and the saints of that day are remembered. The Lord's Prayer and another prayer end the office, then we sit and wait for lunch, or for the afternoon's work.

When I created my own pattern of midday psalms, it made
sense to me to use virtually all the Songs of Ascents, and have
two per day rather than three. This works out as follows:

Monday	120, 121
Tuesday	122, 123
Wednesday	124, 125
Thursday	126, 127
Friday	128, 131
Saturday	133, 150

(You will see that I have left out s few psalms. 129 is about
cursing one's enemies, 130 is used on Wednesdays as
part of morning prayer, 132 is a longish historical psalm which
is used elsewhere).

None of these psalms are longer than 9 verses, some are only
3 verses long. There is always a verse which encourages me
amid the day's stresses, e.g.:

Monday
*The Lord will keep your going out and your
coming in from this time on and for evermore*
(Ps. 121.8)

Tuesday
*As the eyes of servants look to the hand of
their master, as the eyes of a maid look to the
hand of her mistress, so our eyes look to the
Lord our God until he has mercy upon us.*
(Ps. 123.2)

Wednesday
*Our help is in the name of the Lord
who made heaven and earth.* (Ps. 124.8)

Thursday
*May those who sow in tears
reap with shouts of joy.* (Ps. 126.5)

Friday   *Happy is everyone who fears the Lord,*
                who walks in his ways. (Ps. 128.1)

Saturday   *How very good and pleasant it is*
                when kindred live together in unity!
                (Ps.133.1)

I have a small pocket New Testament and Psalms which includes the book of Proverbs. A Kindle will do just as well. Proverbs is an ideal reading for the middle of the working day. It doesn't make great spiritual demands. Instead it reflects on what works and what doesn't work in ordinary life. Some of them are absolutely relevant today, like:

> *To watch over mouth and tongue*
> *is to keep out of trouble. (21.23)*

or: *The clever see danger and hide;*
        but the simple go on and suffer for it.

Conveniently, Proverbs is divided into 31 chapters, one for each day of the month. Each chapter includes about 30 sayings, and I read through them and pick one that makes sense to me that day. For instance, I am writing this on 9th March. A verse I found in chapter 9 was:

> *"The fear of the Lord is the beginning of wisdom,*
> *and the knowledge of the Holy One is insight."*
> *(Proverbs 9:10)*

I end the Midday Prayer by saying the following prayer, from the Community of Taizé in France:

> *Bless us, Lord, now in the middle of the day.*
> *Be with us and with those who are dear to us,*
> *and with everyone we meet.*
> *Keep us in the spirit of the Beatitudes,*
> *joyful, simple, merciful. Amen.*

This little service gives a 5-minute "breather" half way through the working day. It is a definite de-stresser. The whoe of this little service is on the next page. It can be downoaded for free as part of an A5 leaflet on the blog at bibleinbrief.org.

Midday Prayer

Psalms

Monday	120, 121
Tuesday	122, 123
Wednesday	124, 125
Thursday	126, 127
Friday	128, 131
Saturday	133, 150
Sunday	-

Reading a chapter from Proverbs, according to date.

Prayer

> *Bless us, Lord, now in the middle of the day.*
> *Be with us and all who are dear to us*
> *and with everyone we meet.*
> *Keep us in the spirit of the Beatitudes,*
> *joyful, simple, merciful. Amen.*

"The Lord almighty grant us a quiet night and a perfect end"

Common Worship - An Order for Night Prayer

Chapter 6

Compline - completing the day

I t seems that St Benedict, in his Rule, may have invented the office of Compline, or Night Prayer. The word comes from the Latin "completorium" meaning "completion" Chapter 18 of the Rule has this sentence:

"At Compline the same Psalms are to be repeated every day, namely Psalms 4, 90 and 133." - or, in Protestant Bibles, Psalms 4, 91 and 134.

I will use the word Compline here rather than Night Prayer which is the title of the prayer in some modern liturgies. Whatever you call it, it is a wonderful way of closing the day down and getting ready to sleep. I say it most nights. And the core of it is, once again, the Psalms.

Unlike all other Compline services, I do not follow St Benedict's scheme. I find Psalm 139 really speaks to me at night, and so I alternate it with Psalms 91 and use Psalm 134 as an introduction. When these are solidly in my mind, I can spread my wings and add a further twelve psalms, all with a similar theme of trust in God,. They include the traditional night psalm 4. Together they form a fortnightly cycle, mirroring the morning psalms.

Here is my short Compline. It is set out on one side of A5 at the end of the book and can be downloaded on the blog at bibleinbrief.org:

Introduction
The Lord almighty grant us a quiet night and a
perfect end.
O God, make speed to save us.
O Lord, make haste to help us.

Glory to the Father and to the Son
and to the Holy Spirit ;
as it was in the beginning is now
and shall be for ever. Amen.

(Note: "O God, make speed to save us..." is Psalm 70 v.1, taken from the 1535 translation fo the Bible by Miles Coverdale. The Psalms in the Book of Common Prayer, last revised in 1662, are all from Coverdale's translation. The reason why this comes in most of the daily services is the legacy of a 4th century monk, John Cassian. He lived from 360 to 435 and lived in modern Romania, Palestine, Egypt and southern Gaul near Marseilles. He was told by an old monk in Egypt that the secret of continual prayer was reciting this verse. In his book 'Conferences', Cassian says, "It takes up all the emotions that can be applied to human nature and with great correctness and accuracy it adjusts itself to every condition and every attack.")

Psalms
Psalm 134

> *Come bless the Lord, all you servants of the Lord,*
> *who stand by night in the house of the Lord!*
> *Lift up your hands to the holy place,*
> *and bless the Lord.*
> *May the Lord, maker of heaven and earth,*
> *bless you from Zion.*

(Note: this can be said or sung. I know a very simple tune which works for me. You can access it via the blog at bibleinbrief.org)

Psalm 91

> *You who live in the shelter of the Most High,*
> *who abide in the shadow of the Almighty,*
> *will say to the Lord, 'My refuge and my fortress;*
> *my God, in whom I trust.*

Or:

Psalm 139

> *O Lord, you have searched me and known me.*
> *You know when I sit down and when I rise up;*
> *You discern my thoughts for far away ...*
> *If I say "surely the darkness shall cover me,*
> *and the light around me become night',*
> *even the darkness is not dark to you*
> *the night is as bright as the day,*
> *for darkness is as light to you ...*

(Note: I leave out verses 19-22 which are all about hating God's enemies – not quite what Jesus meant when he told us to love our enemies.)

You can also follow a fortnightly course which uses 12 further psalms which can also express a spirit of trust as we go to sleep. These are set out at the end of this chapter. (The Church of England's Common Prayer gives alternative psalms which can be used durinng the week at Night Prayer).

Bible Reading e.g.:

> *You, O Lord, are in the midst of us*
> *and we are called by your name;*
> *leave us not, O Lord our God.*
> (Jeremiah 14.9)

or:

> *Be sober, be vigilant, because your adversary the devil*
> *is prowling round like a roaring lion, seeking for*
> *someone to devour. Resist him, strong in the faith.*
> (1 Peter 5.8,9)

or any other passage of scripture you choose.

(Note: in the traditional prayer of Compline, the verses from 1 Peter come at the very beginning of the service).

Reflecting on the Day

Here I spend a few minutes reflecting on the past day, asking for forgiveness and saying thank you. I usually aim to say thank you for 10 things, one for each finger.

Responses

> *Into your hands, O Lord, I commend my spirit,*
> *for you have redeemed me, Lord, God of truth.*
> (Psalm 31.5)

> *Keep me as the apple of your eye;*
> *hide me under the shadow of your wings.*
> (Psalm 17.8)

Nunc Dimittis (Luke 2.29-32) and response:

> *Save us ,O Lord, while waking,*
> *and guard us while sleeping,*
> *that awake we may watch with Christ,*
> *and asleep may rest in peace.*

(This can be repeated at the end of the Nunc Dimittis).

> *Now, Lord, you let your servant go in peace:*
> *your word has been fulfilled.*
> *My own eyes have seen the salvation*
> *which you have prepared in the sight of every people;*
> *A light to reveal you to the nations*
> *and the glory of your people Israel.*

> *Glory to the Father and to the Son*
> *and to the Holy Spirit ;*
> *as it was in the beginning is now*
> *and shall be for ever. Amen.*

Final Prayer

> *Visit this place, O Lord, we pray.*
> *And drive far from it the snares of the enemy;*
> *may your holy angels dwell with us and guard us*
> *in peace,*
> *and may your blessing be always upon us;*
> *through Jesus Christ our Lord. Amen.*

Spiritual Pest Control

When I was a new curate at St Leonard's Streatham, my vicar, Jeffry Wilcox, sent me out on a somewhat problematic parish visit. A family who did not go to church felt that their house had something spiritually bad in it, and this was seen in the fact that the dad's racing pigeons kept dying. Jeffry said to me, "I don't know quite what you can do. As you're in your first year, you can't do an exorcism or celebrate holy communion. Just try to think of something."

It occurred to me that Compline, especially in its traditional form, was very much about protection from the powers of evil, and no one could object to my saying Compline with the family. So that it is what we did, starting in the living room and saying various psalms in the different rooms of the house. Later I heard that the man's racing pigeons did stop dying for at least six months.

I used to visit a young couple living in a bed-sitting room. They had no church connection; the man had been a member of the Unification Church of Revd Moon – quite cultish - but had already left that. They wanted to get married but could not afford to as they would lose out on benefits, so the woman had changed her name by deed poll. One evening I noticed that they had put up a large wooden cross on the wall above their bed. The reason was that they had been experiencing some very disturbing phenomena, such as a disembodied hand clutching the man's leg in the middle of the night. They linked these phenomena to another man living in the house who had started practising black magic. They had scattered salt around the bed and sprinkled water but nothing had worked. Together we prayed Psalm 91 and the Lord's Prayer; (they repeated each line after me as they did not know it). End of problem! They both started coming to church, the young woman gave her life to Christ and six months later was confirmed.

Saying Compline in places where there was some psychic disturbance became my default *modus operandi*, and it always seemed to bring peace. I was careful to take another Chistian along with me, and if I had not been a vicar I would certainly have consulted one. For instance, in Kingston two young women came to me about a disturbing atmosphere in their bedroom, probably linked to a room downstairs that had been painted black and might well have been used for black magic. They knocked on my door as they were on their way to Brighton to ask a spiritualist medium to come and help. Had they got a spiritualist involved, I would not have gone to their flat; for me, the spiritual vibrations would have been too confused and risky. But since they came to me first, I went along with two other Christians. We said compline and at one point one of the church members with me felt a creepy sensation of something leaving. Saying compline again brought peace.

This all sounds peculiar, but it was put succintly by Dom Robert Petitpierre, a monk who was very experienced in this sort of thing. "It's quite simple really. You say your prayers and the Lord deals with it."

Two Weeks of Psalms

Here are the Psalms I suggest for a fortnightly cycle of psalms. They do not include some of the psalms suggested as a weekly cycle in the Church of England's Common Prayer, because several of those are used here in the morning cycle of psalms.

Or you could choose just one of the weeks and have a weekly cycle. How you use them is entirely up to you.

Week 1	Psalm	
Monday	34 v.7	*O taste and see that the Lord is good; happy are those who take refuge in him.*
Tuesday	30 v.2	*O Lord my God, I cried to you for help, and you have healed me.*
Wednesday	31 v.5/14	*I trust in you, O Lord, I say, "You are my God".*
Thursday	16 v.8	*I keep the Lord always before me; because he is at my right hand, I shall not be moved.*

Friday	42 v.2	*My soul thirsts for God,* *for the living God,* *when shall I come* *and behold the face of God?*
Saturday	4 v.8	*I will both lie down and sleep in* *peace;* *for you alone, O Lord,* *make me lie down in safety.*
Sunday	91 v.9	*Because you have made the Lord* *your refuge,* *the Most High your dwelling place,* *no evil shall befall you,* *no scourge come near your tent.*

Week 2   **Psalm**

Monday	56 v.4	*In God whose word I praise,* *in God I trust;* *I am not afraid,* *what can flesh do to me?*
Tuesday	62 v.1	*For God alone my soul waits in* *silence;* *from him comes my salvation.*
Wednesday	71 v.1, 2	*In you, O Lord, I take refuge;* *let me never be put to shame.* *In your righteousness deliver me* *and rescue me;* *incline your ear to me and save me.*
Thursday	116 v.7	*Return, O my soul, to your rest,* *for the Lord has dealt bountifully* *with you.*

Friday	43 v.5	*Why are you cast down, O my soul, and why are you disquieted within me?*
		Hope in God; for I shall again praise him,
		my help and my God.

| Saturday | 3 v.5 | *I lie down and sleep;* |
| | | *I wake again, for the Lord sustains me.* |

(Note: When St Jerome (347-420 AD) was asked by a father how he could teach his young son to pray, he replied, "Start with Psalm 3").

| Sunday | 139 | *If I take the wings of the morning and settle at the farthest limit of the sea,* |
| | | *even there your hand shall lead me, and your right hand shall hold me fast.* |

Compline (or Night Prayer)

The Lord almighty grant us a quiet night and a
perfect end.
O God make speed to save us.
O Lord make haste to help us.

Psalms
Psalms 134, then 91 or 139 (omit verses 19-22)
For other psalms, see over.

Bible Reading
e. g. Jeremiah 14.9, 1 Peter 5.8,9 or Revelation 22.4,5
or some other Bible passage.

Reflection on the day
Confession and thanksgiving

Response
Into your hands I commend my spirit,
you have redeemed me O Lord, you God of truth.
Keep me as the apple of your eye;
hide me under the shelter of your wings.

The Nunc Dimittis (Luke 2.29-32)
Save us, O Lord, while waking,
watch over us while sleeping;
that awake we may watch with Christ,
and asleep we may rest in peace. (repeated at end)

Lord, now you let your servant go in peace,
your word has been fulfilled.
My own eyes have seen the salvation
which you have prepared in the sight of every people;

A light to reveal you to the nations
and the glory of your people Israel.

Glory to the Father and to the Son and to the Holy Spirit;
as it was in the beginning, is now,and shall be for ever.
Amen.

Final prayer

Visit this place, O Lord, we pray,
and drive far from it the snares of the enemy;
may your holy angels dwell here and guard us in peace,
and may your blessing be always upon us;
through Jesus Christ our Lord.
Amen.

Psalms

	Week 1	Week 2
Monday	34	56
Tuesday	30	62
Wednesday	31	71
Thursday	16	116
Friday	42	43 or 88
Saturday	4	3
Sunday	91	139

"A serious house on serious earth it is."

Philip Larkin "Church Going"

Chapter 7

Church on Sunday

When I was vicar at Hackbridge and Beddington Corner (between Croydon and Sutton), I started a very simple way of praying with the churchwardens and others before the main Sunday service. It had to be very simple, because there were always scores of practical things to get sorted out beforehand, and however well organised I had been in advance (usually not very), something always seemed to happen to throw a spanner in the works at the last minute. So I devised a very short prayer based on one particular psalm, Psalm 84:

"A people without the knowledge of their past history, origin and culture is like a tree without roots."

Marcus Garvey, Jamaican political leader

Chapter 8

And the rest: History and Wisdom

You may have worked out that despite using a great number of psalms in the morning, at lunchtime and at night, 87 of the 150 are still unaccounted for. We have only used 42%. The remaining 58% include the excessively long Psalm 119 (176 verses!) and all the bloodthirsty ones, raining down curses on one's enemies. Can we do anything at all with these? I decided to liberate my inner geek and have a go.

History

To my astonishment I found that all the violent psalms could be fitted easily into a four-week pattern, each week going through the history of Israel:

- Exodus, the deliverance from Egypt;
- the conquest of Canaan;
- the 400 years which witnessed the prosperity and decline of the twin kingdoms of Israel and Judah;
- the destruction first of Israel, the northern kingdom in 722 BC, followed by the destruciton of Jerusalem in 587 BC;
- the exile in Babylon and the hope of return.

They also fitted roughly into four elements which made up Hebrew history:

- Judah (the southern kingdom),
- Zion/Jerusalem (the capital of Judah and site of Solomon's Temple),
- Israel (the northern kingdom), and
- David (the ancestor of all the kings of Judah).

Once some shorter psalms are brought together, and two long psalms are split in two, they give a clear four week framework. Here is how it works for the first week, focussing on Judah, the southern kingdom:

Monday   **Exodus**
Psalm 105   Tells the story of Genesis and Exodus, from Abraham through Joseph to the plagues of Egypt and the 40 years wandering in the desert.

Tuesday **Conquest**
Psalm 68 *Let God arise, let his enemies be scattered;*
let those who hate him flee before him. (68.1)

Wednesday **The Kingdom**
Psalms 2 & 72 *"I have set my king on Zion, my holy hill." (2.6)*
For he delivers the needy when they call,
the poor and those who have no helper.
(72.12)

Thursday **Decline**
Psalms 82 & 60 *"How long will you judged unjustly*
and show partiality to the wicked.?" (82.2)

Friday **Disaster**
Psalm 79 *O God, the nations have come into your*
inheritance;
they have defiled your holy temple,
they have laid Jeruslaem in ruins. (79.1)

Saturday **Exile and Return**
Psalms 83 & 87 *They say, 'Come, let us wipe them out as*
a nation, let the name of Israel be
remembered no more. (83.4)
Of Zion it will be said,
"This one and that one were born in her",
for the Most High himself will establish it.
(87.5)

Highlights from the remaining three weeks include:

Zion/Jerusalem
Conquest: Psalm 132
"Rise up, O Lord, and go to your resting place,
you and the ark of your might...
For the Lord has chosen Zion,
he has desired it for his habitation."
(132.8,13)

Destruction: Psalm 74
Direct your steps to the perpetual ruins;
the enemy has destroyed everything in the sanctuary.
They set your sanctuary on fire;
they burned all the meeting-places of God in the land.
(74.3,7,8)

Exile and return: Psalm 137
By the waters of Babylon -
there we sat down and wept
when we remembered Zion.
O daughter of Babylon, you devastator!
Happy shall they be who take your little ones
and dash them against the rock!"

Israel (The Northern Kingdom)
(Note, Israel is also referred to as Ephraim, Jacob and Joseph).
Conquest: Psalm 46
The kingdoms are in an uproar, the kingdoms totter;
he utters his voice, the earth melts.
The Lord of hosts is with us,
the God of Jacob is our refuge
(46.6,7)

Kingdom: Psalm 45
In your majesty ride on victoriously
for the cause of truth and to defend the right.
From ivory palaces stringed instruments make you glad ...
at your right hand stands the queen in gold of Ophir. (45.4,8,9)

Decline: Psalm 78
When God heard, he was full of wrath,
and he utterly rejected Israel.
He abandoned his dwelling at Shiloh ...
and delivered his power to captivity. (78.59,60,61)

David - the ancestor of all the kings of Judah
Exodus: Psalm 18
He reached down from on high, he took me,
he drew me out of mighty waters.
He delivered me from my strong enemy,
and from those who hated me. (18.16)

Conquest: Psalm 18
I pursued my enemies and overtook them;
and did not turn back till they were consumed. (18.37)

Kingdom: Pslam 89
Once and for all I have sworn my my holiness;
I will not lie to David'
His line shall continue for ever,
and his throne endure before me like the sun. (18.36,37)

Decline: Psalm 89
But you have rejected, you have spurned,
you are full of wrath against your anointed.
You have renounced the covenant with your servant;
you have defiled his crown in the dust.   (89.38,39)

Exile and return: Psalm 85
Lord, You were favourable to your land;
you restored the fortunes of Jacob.
Surely his salvation is at hand for those who fear him,
that his glory may dwell in our land. (85.1)

Wisdom, The Law and Laments

Wisdom is a category of literature in the Bible, indeed all over
the ancient world, which was concerned with how we can live
well. The books of of the Bible which are prime examples are
Job, Proverbs, Ecclesiastes and many of the Psalms, over
170 pages.

The key wisdom book is Proverbs. Proverbs is a long collection
of mostly two-line sayings on how to achieve prosperity and
peace in life, e.g.

> *To guarantee loans for a stranger brings trouble,*
> *but there is safety in refusing to do so.*
> *The people curse those who hold back grain (to increase*
> *the price),*
> *but a blessing is on the head of those who sell it.*
> *(Proverbs 11.15, 26)*

In Israel there was a fundamentally ethical view of the
good life, rooted in obedience to the Law or Torah – the
commandments given to the Hebrews during their desert
wanderings after leaving Egypt. These come in the books of
Exodus, Leviticus, Numbers and Deuteronomy. Keeping the
commandments was the way one entered into a relationship
with God and received his guidance. This is how Proverbs
understands wisdom.

> *If you indeed cry out for insight*
> *and raise your voice for understanding*
> *then you will understand the fear of the Lord,*
> *and find the knowledge of God.*
> (Proverbs 2.3,5)

Ecclesiastes has a similar agenda of worldly contentment but comes to it from an effectively agnostic point of view, and with fairly despairing conclusions:

> *Then I remembered all that my hands had done*
> *and the toil I had spent in doing it,*
> *and again, all was vanity and a chasing after wind.*
> (Ecclesiastes 2.11)

This attitude leads to the theme of undeserved suffering, which is the subject of the book of Job. Job agonises over the question of why God allows undeserved suffering and does nothing about it. In particular why do the wicked seem to prosper?

The same theme is there strongly in the Psalms, like the verse which Jesus quoted on the cross, *"My God, my God, why have you forsaken me?"* (Psalm 22.1)

There are several psalms which reflect on this, e.g.
> *I was envious of the arrogant;*
> *I saw the prosperity of the wicked...*
> *But when I thought how to understand this,*
> *it seemed to me a wearisome task,*
> *until I went to the sanctuary of God;*
> *then I perceived their end.* (Psalm 73.3,16,17)

It is not just an intellectual argument which we see in the Psalms, but the cry of wounded hearts. Laments are as common in the Psalms as songs of praise. The bleakest is Psalm 88, which, unlike all other psalms, ends without a ray of hope:

Your wrath has swept over me,
your dread assaults destroy me...
You have caused friend and neighbour to shun me;
my companions are in darkness. (Psalm 88.16,18)

They also acknowledge frankly that evil does exist, and that God is not indifferent:

Their mouths are filled with cursing and deceit
and oppression;
under their tongues are mischief and iniquity.
(Psalm 10.7)

God is a righteous judge,
and a God who has indignation every day. (Psalm 7.11)

A thought in which I find some comfort.

The course of psalms for the last four weeks is made up of all these kinds of Wisdom Psalms. Central to them is the faith that following God's commandments in the Law is the way to a life of contentment. This is especially so of Psalm 119.

The whole of Psalm 119 is a worshipful meditation on the Law. It is an acrostic poem, each set of eight verses is made up of lines starting with the same letter of the alphabet: aleph, beth, gimel etc. And since there are 22 letters in the Hebrew alphabet, Psalm 119 has 176 verses.

> *Happy are those whose way is blameless,*
> *who walk in the law of the Lord.*
> *Happy are those who keep his decrees,*
> *who seek him with their whole heart.* (Psalm 119.1,2)

My suggestion is that one of each of the 22 sections of 8 verses is read each day. The two days remaining use Psalms 1 and 19 as an introduction.

Psalm 1 starts the whole book of Psalms with:
> *Happy are those who do not follow the advice of*
> *the wicked,*
> *or take the path that sinners tread,*
> *or sit in the seat of scoffers;*
> *But their delight is in the law of the lord,*
> *and on his law they meditate day and night.*
> (Psalm 1.1,2)

Psalm 19 is a great song of praise about the Law:
> *The law of the Lord is perfect, reviving the soul;*
> *the decrees of the Lord are sure, making wise*
> *the simple.* (Psalm 19.7)

Five psalms, 8, 29, 104, 147 and 148, praise God specifically for his work in creating the world. These are set for the Monday of each week.

> You set the earth on its foundations,
> so that it shall never be shaken.
> You make springs gush forth in the valleys;
> they flow between the hills.
> O Lord, how manifold are your works!
> In wisdom you have made them all;
> the earth is full of your creatures. (Psalm 104. 5,10,24)

The rest of the psalms, primarily wisdom and lament psalms, are allocated in numerical order, aiming at roughly the same number of verses each day.

I have left out three psalms which are duplicated elsewhere in the book, e.g. 14=53; 70=40.13-17; 108=57.7-11 + 60.5-12. And I have excluded psalms which are primarily about cursing one's enemies, on the basis that to hold resentments against others is like drinking poison and expecting the other person to fall down dead. Those not appearing are: 58, 59, 109; 129; 140.

The listing of all these psalms according to weeks and days is set out on pages 87-88.

It is all very well having worked out how one could theoretically allocate these 79 psalms, but how and why should one actually use them?

This is where I come to confession time. I confess that having worked out this scheme, I have hardly used it. This is because I tend to be a workaholic; to create a space at the end of the working day to stop and turn my attention to God is something I find quite difficult. Others may well be more disciplined and better at getting their priorities right than I do. Or perhaps if you have a long commute by train after work it could become of your going home routine. However, I can see myself using them a part of a very simple evening prayer made up as follows;

1   Evening hymn: Hail gladdening light.
This is the most ancient Christian hymn we have, written in
Greek around 300 AD. It was sung at the lighting of lamps
at the evening service. I love the version by John Keble with
music by John Stainer, very serene. It can be accessed on the
blog at bibleinbrief.org or on youtube.com.

2   Traditional Evening Psalm – Psalm 141
O Lord, I call to you; come to me quickly;
hear my voice when I cry to you.
Let my prayer come before you as incense,
the lifting up of my hands as the evening sacrifice.

3   Psalms

4   Meditation ending with the Lord's Prayer
 (I have not included a Bible reading because I think that after
some longish psalms, we may well have had enough
Scripture input).

5   (optional)
A New Testament Canticle (which means the same as Psalm,
but from the New Testament instead of the Old Testament)

Monday
Magnificat – Luke 2.46-55; the song of Mary
My soul magnifies the Lord
and my spirit rejoices in God my Saviour,
for he has looked with favour on the lowliness of
his servant,
surely from now on all generations will call me blessed...

Tuesday
Benedictus – Luke 2.68-79; the song of Zechariah
> *Blessed be the Lord God of Israel*
> *for he has looked favourably on his people and*
> *redeemed them.*
> *He has raised a mighty saviour for us*
> *in the house of his servant David...*

Wednesday
The Beatitudes – Matthew 5.3-10
> *Blessed are the poor in spirit, for theirs is the kingdom*
> *of heaven.*
> *Blessed are those who mourn, for they will be*
> *comforted.*
> *Blessed are the meek, for they will inherit the earth.*
> *Blessed are those who hunger and thirst after*
> *righteousness,*
> *for they will be filled...*

Thursday
The Song of Christ's Glory – Philippians 2.5-11
> *Let the same mind be in you that was in Christ Jesus,*
> *who, though he was in the form of God*
> *did not regard equality with God as somethng to*
> *be exploited,*
> *but emptied himself, taking the form of a slave...*

Friday
The Suffering of Christ – 1 Peter 2.22-25
> *He committed no sin,*
> *and no deceit was found in his mouth.*
> *When he was abused, he did not return abuse;*
> *when he suffered he did not threaten...*

Saturday

The Glory Beyond – Revelation 4.11, 5.9-14

You are worthy, O Lord and God,
to receive glory ad honour and power,
for you created all things,
and by your will they existed and were created...

6   Final prayer (From the Church of North India)

Lord Jesus, stay with us,
for the day is passing and the evening is at hand;
be our companion on the way,
kindle our heart with love and joy,
and let us know you in your risen power,
for you are our Lord and our God. Amen.

The whole Evening Prayer is set out on one page overleaf, with the psalms on the next two pages. It can be downloaded as an A5 leaflet on the blog at bibleinbrief.org.

Evening Prayer

Hymn

> Hail, gladdening Light, of his pure glory poured,
> Who is the immortal Father, heavenly, blest,
> Holiest of holies, Jesus Christ, our Lord.
>
> Now we have come to the sun's hour of rest,
> The lights of evening round us shine,
> We hymn the Father, Son and Holy Spirit divine.
>
> Worthiest art thou at all times to be sung
> With undefiléd tongue,
> Son of our God, Giver of life, alone!
> Therefore in all the world thy glories, Lord, they own.

Response

> O Lord, I call to you; come to me quickly;
> hear my voice when I cry to you.
> Let my prayer come before you as incense,
> the lifting up of my hands as the evening sacrifice.
> (Psalm 141.1,2)

Psalms see pages 45 and 46.

Meditation
Ending with the Lord's Prayer

New Testament Canticle (optional)

Monday	Magnificat:	Luke 2.46-55; the song of Mary
Tuesday	Benedictus:	Luke 2.68-79; the song of Zechariah
Wednesday	The Beatitudes:	Matthew 5.3-10
Thursday	Song of Christ's Glory:	Philippians 2.5-11
Friday	The Suffering of Christ:	1 Peter 2.21-25
Saturday	The Glory Beyond:	Revelation 4.11, 5.9-14

Concluding prayer

Lord Jesus, stay with us,
for the day is passing and the evening is at hand;
be our companion on the way,
kindle our heart with love and joy,
and let us know you in your risen power,
for you are our Lord and our God. Amen.

Evening Prayer 1
Historical Psalms

		Week 1 Judah	Week 2 Zion
Monday	Exodus	105	114, 135
Tuesday	Conquest	68	132, 110
Wednesday	Kingdom	2, 72	20, 21, 48
Thursday	Decline	82, 60	9, 76
Friday	Disaster	79	74
Saturday	Exile & Return	83, 87	137, 126

		Week 3 Israel	Week 4 David
Monday	Exodus	106	18.1-30
Tuesday	Conquest	46, 47	18.31-50
Wednesday	Kingdom	45, 101	89.1-37
Thursday	Decline	78.1-16	89.34-51 52-72
Friday	Disaster	80	44
Saturday	Exile & Return	81	85

Note: The verse numbers are taken from an ordinary Bible. In "Common Prayer" and similar church worship books they differ slightly.

Evening Prayer 2
Wisdom Psalms

	Week 1	Week 2
Monday	1 + 8, 29	119.33-40 + 104
Tuesday	19 + 5, 7, 10	" 41-48 + 39, 41
Wednesday	119.1-8 + 11, 12, 13, 15	" 49-56 + 49
Thursday	" 9-16 + 24, 26, 28	" 57-64 + 50
Friday	" 17-24 + 35	" 65-72 + 52, 53, 54
Saturday	" 25-32 + 37	" 73-80 + 55, 57

	Week 3	Week 4
Monday	119.81-88 + 147	119.129-136 + 94
Tuesday	" 89-96 + 64, 65	" 137-144 + 94
Wednesday	" 97-104 + 73	" 145-152 + 107
Thursday	" 105-112 + 61, 75	" 153-160 + 111, 112, 115
Friday	" 113-120 + 77	" 161-168 + 141, 142
Saturday	" 121-128 + 90, 92	" 169-176 + 144, 149

"To read the Bible is of itself a laudable occupation."

John Quincy Adams, President of the United States 1826-1829

Chapter 9

Bible Reading Suggestions

I suggest that some portion of the Bible is read at Morning Prayer and at Compline, and possibly at Evening Prayer. At Midday Prayer a chapter of Proverbs has already been suggested. One way of reading in the morning or at night is to start at Genesis and go on to the end – not recommended. Or opening a Bible at random and reading what one's eye falls on – equally not recommended. So what can we do?

There are loads of guides we can choose from. Here are a few.

The Church of England Lectionary

This is a small 80 page booklet which provides readings for the church, published annually. It costs £4.99. Don't use the Kindle version – the print is tiny. (Note: the church year starts at Advent, around 27th November, about four weeks before Christmas, not on 1st January).

It is particularly useful, because it gives you a choice of four different reading schemes, with all of them having readings from both the Old Testament and the New Testament.

The first column is readings for daily Holy Communion. These always include a short reading from Matthew, Mark, Luke or John, typically between four and a dozen verses, together with another reading either from the Old Testament or from one of the New Testament Letters of the same length. For instance, today, 21st March, the readings are Daniel 2.20-23 and Matthew 18.21-end. Sometimes these readings go through a book of the Bible consecutively. Sometimes, for example during Christmas and Lent, they dodge around, expressing the theme of the church season.

The next two columns are for Morning and Evening Prayer. These are longer readings. One of the New Testament readings is always from a Gospel, read either in the morning or at evening. They always follow the particular book in order, except when interrupted by a saint's day, In which case I used to work out which passages were being missed out and read those. My practice is to use the Morning Prayer readings, the New Testament in the morning and the Old Testament later in the day. So for example, the readings for 21st March are: Jeremiah 11.18 – 12.6 and John 8.12-30 for morning prayer, and Genesis 47.28 – 48. and Hebrews 5.11 – 6.12 for evening prayer.

If you feel that these are a bit stringent, there is another scheme at the back of the book, p. 70ff, the Additional Weekday Lectionary. These readings, from Old and New Testaments, are between 5 and 12 verses long, and are chosen fairly randomly. If you feel that your Bible reading is getting a bit jaded, this is quite a good option, because you never know what will turn up.

Bible Reading Fellowship

The Bible Readng Fellowship (or BRF) has been producing notes for Bible reading for almost a century. "Since we began in 1922, our vision has been to encourage people to explore and understand the Bible, enjoy a deeper experience of prayer and apply what they learn to their lives day by day." All their booklets cover four months.

New Daylight
A short Bible passage is printed out, followed by a comment and a prayer or reflection

Guidelines
An in-depth study with insights from current scholarship. The units are not dated but each week is split into six sections. You need a Bible alongside.

Day by Day with God
Written with women in mind, each day has a Bible passage with a key verse written out and a comment explaining the passage.

The Upper Room
All the meditations are written by the readers themselves. You will need a Bible for the passage and the key verse. Over 3 million readers worldwide!

More details are on the websites brf.org.uk or biblereadingnotes.org.uk

Crusade for World Revival
Selwyn Hughes was a South Wales coal miner who felt called by God to become a minister. In 1965 he founded Crusade for World Revival (CWR) and began writing a daily devotional called "Every Day With Jesus" It now has about half a million readers. Five daily reading notes for adults are now published on a two-monthly basis:

Every Day with Jesus: a brief text, a comment applying it to life and a prayer.

Cover to Cover Every Day: a more in-depth study of two books of the Bible each month, one Old Testament, one New Testament, and a psalm each weekend.

Inspiring Women Every Day: written by women for women.

Life Every Day: life application notes by Jeff Lucas.

The Manual: written by men for men.

All these are available at cwr.org.uk

Our Daily Bread Ministries
Our Daily Bread Ministries started in 1938 as a radio programme called Detroit Bible Class. They now distribute over 60 million resources to 150 countries. "Regardless of whether it's a radio or television broadcast, DVD, podcast, book, mobile app, or website, we provide materials to help people grow in their relationship with God."

Our Daily Bread is a free daily devotional based on a Bible verse each day, with other suggestions for reading. I found it simple and sane. The website is odb.org

Bible in Brief

This is a six month, undated, comprehensive overview of the Bible. It has a separate theme for each month: Genesis & Exodus; History of Israel and Judah; the Prophets; Law, Psalms and Wisdom; Jesus; Apostles and their Letters. And each week has a separate theme, so you can choose the part of the Bible which interests you. At the end of each month is a section called "The Other Side", which gives extracts from writings of the surrounding cultures. For instance, after the first month there are extracts from the Babylonian creation myth and from the account of the flood in the Epic of Gilgamesh. Each day has a question to which you can respond in the book itself or on a discussion forum online at bibleinbrief.org. You can also get it delivered to your email.

"Long ago ago God spoke to our ancestors in many and various ways by the prophets…"

Hebrews 1.1

Chapter 10

Who wrote what when

This will be a very short chapter.

Who wrote the Psalms?   We don't know.
What are the Psalms? Religious poetry written in Hebrew.
When were they written? Probably between 1000 BC and
300 BC.

But, you may ask, didn't King David write all of them?

We don't know. It is true that 116 of the Psalms have a heading, like:

"For the director of music. According to gittith. A psalm of David." (Psalm 8). Of these, 73 psalms are ascribed to David, and Psalm 72 concludes with "The prayers of David son of Jesse are ended." Other names mentioned at the head of various psalms are Asaph (12), the sons of Korah (11), Soloman (2), Moses (1) and Heman (1). Asaph and the sons of Korah were singers in the Temple in David's time (See Chronicles 6).

It may be that "a psalm of David" means a psalm used by the king during the period of the monarchy. It could mean a collection of psalms reflecting the time of David, just as we would refer to Elizabethan music in the time of Shakespeare. Some might go back to David himself, whose musicianship was famous.

In brief, the writing of the psalms could come in three periods:
a) the monarchy, before the exile. Some may go back to the time of David, some may have been used by the king at the time during festivals in the Temple.
b) during the exile in Babylon; psalms which lament the destruction of Jeruslaem clearly belong here.
c) on return from exile; This may have been the time when the Psalms were collected together in the form we now have them – though there are slight differences in the division of psalms between the Septuagint, c, 280-250 BC and the Hebrew Psalms in the Dead Sea Scrolls, c. 0 AD. Some new psalms may have been written during this period. Perhaps the headings were added at this time.

If you want to explore further, try Wikipedia.

One thing I am convinced of. All the scholarly guesses in the world do not help us to use the psalms as prayer. We may spend weeks studying about the internal combustion engine, but in fact, cars were made to be driven.

"Long ago ago God spoke to our ancestors in many and various ways by the prophets…"

Hebrews 1.1

Chapter 11

Sing something simple

The word Psalm probably meant singing to a stringed instrument, but it is clear that in the Temple it included all sorts of instruments:

Praise him with trumpet sound;
praise him with lute and harp!
Praise him with tambourine and dance;
praise him with strings and pipe!
Praise him with clanging cymbals;
praise him loud clashing cymbals!
(Psalm 150,3-5)

So if you play an instrument, including percussion, feel free to set the psalms to music!

However, for prayer I think we need something quieter. The songs of Taizé are a treasure house of simple worship chants which can be sung repetitively. They came about because when the little community started having young people travel to them from all over Europe and the world, they had to find a style of worship which was accessible to people of many different languages. Their website, taize.fr, is fascinating. You can experience their songs on youtube. The album "O Lord hear my prayer" is a good one to start with as seven of the songs are in English.

Over the years I have written a few chants myself, and I offer them here in case anyone might like them. They are available on the blog at bibleinbrief.org

> *O God make speed to save me.*
> *O Lord make haste to help me.* (Psalm 71.12)

> *My heart says, Seek his face,*
> *My heart says, Seek his face,*
> *Your face, Lord, do I seek,*
> *Your face, Lord, do I seek.*

> *Hide not your face from me,*
> *Hide not your face from me,*
> *For you, Lord, do I wait,*
> *For you, Lord, do I wait.* (Psalm 27.8,9,14)

In the 1970's, I wrote the following. It shows its age, becaue it uses the 1535 translation from the Book of Common Prayer, but I still like it.

O tarry thou the Lord's leisure,
O tarry thou the Lord's leisure,
Be strong, and he shall comfort thy heart,
Be strong, and he shall comfort thy heart.

O tarry thou the Lord's leisure,
O tarry thou the Lord's leisure,
And put thou thy trust in the Lord,
And put thou thy trust in the Lord. (Psalm 27.14)

One further chant does not come from a psalm, but it is in Hebrew, the language the Psalms were sung in. It is a worship song addressed to God, Father, Son and Spirit. You can hear it on the blog at bibleinbrief.org.

Abba Eloheynu,
Yeshua Adonai
Ruach ha'Kodesh
Hallelu Jah

which means:
Father, our God
Jesus Lord
Holy Spirit
Praise the Lord

Note: Yeshua was the actual name of Jesus. The New Testament was written in Greek and there are no letters in Greek for the sound 'sh'. The normal Greek ending '-ous' was then added on.

The 'ch' in Ruach (spirit or wind) is pronounced like the Scottish 'loch'.

Chapter 12

And finally

There have been lots of suggestions in this book. I think you would be a bit compulsive if you said yes to all of them. My advice is, cherry pick as much as you like. As they say in Alcoholics Anonymous, take what you like and leave the rest.

And bear in mind that words, whether our own or from church tradition or even from the Bible, can only bring us to the threshold of prayer. It is when we encounter something completely mysterious that we start getting close. St Paul has a great passage in Romans:

"Likewise the Spirit helps us in our weakness; for we do not know how to pray as we ought, but that very Spirit intercedes with sighs too deep for words. And God, who searches the heart, knows what is in the mind of the Spirit, because the Spirit intercedes for the saints according to the will of God." (Romans 8.26,27).

Lightning Source UK Ltd.
Milton Keynes UK
UKOW05f0219190417
299424UK00001B/16/P